WITHDRAWN

The Flowering Plant Division

The Flowering Plant Division

REBECCA STEFOFF

Marshall Cavendish
Benchmark
New York

With thanks to Mark Tebbitt, Ph.D., Botanist, Brooklyn Botanic Garden, for his expert
review of the manuscript

Marshall Cavendish Benchmark
99 White Plains Road
Tarrytown, New York 10591-9001
www.marshallcavendish.us

Library of Congress Cataloging-in-Publication Data
Stefoff, Rebecca, date.
The flowering plant division / by Rebecca Stefoff.— 1st ed.
p. cm. — (Family trees)
Includes bibliographical references and index.
ISBN 0-7614-1817-2
1. Plants—Juvenile literature. 2. Angiosperms—Juvenile literature. I.Title. II. Series.

QK49.S74745 2005
580—dc22
2004021817

Front cover: A cactus flower; Title page: Hummingbird and hibiscus; Back cover: Venus Flytrap
Photo research by Linda Sykes Picture Research
The photographs in this book are used by permission and through the courtesy of: *Plant Kingdom Family Tree:*
Dr. Jeremy Burgess/ Photo Researchers, Inc.: 14 top left; William M. Partington, Jr./Photo Researchers, Inc.: 14
bottom left; TH Foto-Werbung/Photo Researchers, Inc.: 14 top middle; Michael Gadomski/Animals,
Animals-Earth Scenes: 14 bottom right; Michael Gadomski/Animals, Animals-Earth Scenes: 14 top right;
Nature's Images/Photo Researchers, Inc.: 15 bottom left; Ed Reschke/Peter Arnold, Inc.: 15 top left; Scott
Smith/Animals, Animals- Earth Scenes: 15 bottom middle; Jack Wilburn/Animals, Animals- Earth Scenes: 15
top right; Geoff Bryant/Photo Researchers, Inc.: bottom right. *All other credits:* Bill Ross/Corbis: cover; Jany
Sauvanet/Photo Researchers, Inc.: 3, 60; Adam Jones/Visuals Unlimited: 6; Natural History Museum Picture
Library, London, UK: 9; Alan & Linda Detrick/Photo Researchers, Inc.: 12 left; David Schleser/Nature's
Images/ Photo Researchers, Inc.: 12 right; George H. H. Huey/Corbis: 16; Andrew Syred/Photo Researchers,
Inc.: 19, 59; Han Steur/Visuals Unlimited: 21; Ken Lucas/Visuals Unlimited: 22; Henryk T. Kaiser/Index
Stock: 25; Missouri Botanical Garden: 26; David Dilcher: 27; Ted Streshinsky/Corbis: 28; Pat O'Hara/Corbis:
28; Dwight Kuhn: 32. 44, 64; Science VU/Visuals unlimited: 35; Dr. Robert Calentine/Visuals Unlimited: 36;
Picturequest: 37; Clouds Hill Imaging Ltd. /Corbis: 38; Dr. Richard Kessel & Dr. Gene Shih/Visuals Unlimited:
39; Rod Planck/Photo Researchers, Inc.: 41; Francesc Muntada/Corbis: 43; Botanica/Getty Images: 45; Joe &
Mary Ann McDonald/Visuals Unlimited: 46; Richard Hamilton Smith/Corbis: 47; George H. H. Huey/Corbis:
48; Charles Mauzy/Corbis: 49; Carlyn Iverson/Photo Researchers, Inc: 50; Kjell B. Sandved/ Photo
Researchers, Inc.: 51; John Kaprielian/ Photo Researchers, Inc.: 52, 53; Hal Horwitz/Corbis: 54; Kevin and
Betty Collins/Visuals Unlimited: 57; Taxi/Getty Images: 61;Nature's Images/ Photo Researchers, Inc.: 65 left;
Geoff Bryant/Photo Researchers, Inc.: 65 right; Richard Shiell/ Animals, Animals-Earth Scenes: 66;
Robert van der Hilst/Corbis: 68; Peter Johnson/Corbis: 69 left; Eygptian Museum, Cairo, Egypt/Scala/Art
Resource, NY: 69 right; Michael P. Gadomski/Photo Researchers, Inc.: 70; Eric and David Hosking/Corbis: 73;
David R. Frazier/Photo Researchers, Inc.: 75; Will & Deni McIntyre/Corbis: 76; Ron Sanford/Corbis: 77;
Reuters/Corbis: 78; Kevin Schafer/Corbis: 79; Goetgheluck/Peter Arnold: back cover.

Printed in Malaysia
Book design by Patrice Sheridan
3 5 6 4 2

CONTENTS

In the hill country of Texas, live oak trees shade a carpet of paintbrush wildflowers. Both the trees and the wildflowers belong to the largest division of plants in the world today, the angiosperms or flowering plants.

Classifying Life

Picture three plants. The first is a leafy, broad-branched oak tree. The second is a towering pine tree. The third is a duckweed, a tiny plant that floats on ponds. Now imagine that a botanist, who specializes in the study of plants, walks onto the scene and tells you that scientists group two of these plants together in the same category. The third belongs to a different category. How do you think the plants are divided? The two sturdy trees must belong together, leaving the duckweed in a different group—right? Wrong. The oak tree and the duckweed belong together in a category called angiosperms, or flowering plants, while the pine tree belongs to a different category, the gymnosperms.

Our usual idea of a flower is a rose, a tulip, or some other colorful bloom, not an oak tree or a duckweed. A flowering plant, however, is not the same thing as a flower. A flower is simply the reproductive organ of a flowering plant. All angiosperms have flowers, but in many species the flowers are small and almost invisible. The blossom-producing plants that we call "flowers" when we see them in gardens, windowboxes, and vases are angiosperms, but so are grasses, herbs, and most trees and shrubs.

THE INVENTION OF TAXONOMY

To understand why such a wide variety of plants are grouped together as angiosperms, it helps to know something about how scientists classify living things. Science provides tools for making sense of the natural world. One of the most powerful tools is classification, which means organizing things in a pattern according to their differences and similarities. Since ancient times, scientists who study plants and animals have been working to develop taxonomy, a classification system for living things. Taxonomy groups together plants or animals that share certain features, and sets them apart from other plants and animals with different features. Each group is then divided into smaller subgroups, and these in turn are split into still smaller groups. For example, plants form one group and animals form another group. The plant group contains many smaller categories, such as mosses, ferns, and flowering plants. Each of these categories, in turn, contains smaller categories. Taxonomic classification moves from the largest, most inclusive category to the smallest category, which includes just a single species, or type.

The idea behind taxonomy is simple, but the world of living things is complex and full of surprises. Taxonomy is not a fixed pattern. It keeps changing to reflect new knowledge or ideas. Over time, scientists have developed rules for adjusting that pattern even when they occasionally disagree on its details.

One of the first taxonomists was the ancient Greek philosopher Aristotle (384-322 B.C.E.), who investigated many branches of science, including biology. Aristotle arranged living things on a sort of ladder. At the bottom were those he considered lowest, or least developed, such as worms. Above them were things he considered higher, or more developed, such as fish, then birds, then mammals.

For centuries after Aristotle, taxonomy changed very little. People who studied nature tended to classify organisms using obvious features, such as separating trees from grasses or birds from fish. However, they did not try to develop a system for classifying all life. Then, between 1682 and 1705, an English naturalist named John Ray published a plan of the living world that was designed to have a place for every species of plant and animal. Ray's system had several levels of larger and smaller categories. It was the foundation of modern taxonomy.

Swedish naturalist Carolus Linnaeus (1707-1778) built on that foundation to create the taxonomic system used today. Linnaeus was chiefly interested in plants, but his system of classification included all living things. The highest level of classification was the kingdom. To Linnaeus, everything belonged to either the plant or the animal kingdom. Each of these kingdoms was divided into a number of smaller categories called classes. Each class was divided into orders. Each order was divided into genera. Each genus (the singular form of genera) contained one or more species.

Linnaeus also developed another of Ray's ideas: a method for naming species. Before Linnaeus published his important work *System of Nature* in 1735, scientists had no standardized system for referring to plants and animals. Organisms were generally known by their common names,

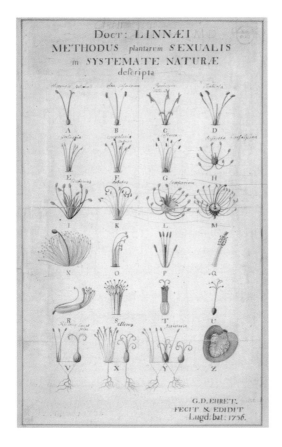

A page from the 1736 book *Systema Naturae*, or *System of Nature*, shows how Carolus Linnaeus of Sweden studied plants' reproductive features as part of classifying the plants into groups.

but many of them had different common names in different countries. As a result, naturalists around the world often called the same type of plant or animal by different names. Sometimes they used the same name to refer to different organisms. Linnaeus wanted to end such confusion and allow scholars everywhere to communicate clearly when writing about plants and animals. He established the practice of giving each plant or animal a scientific name consisting of its genus and species. This binomial, or two-part name, system used Latin, the scientific language of Linnaeus's day, or occasionally Greek. For example, the white oak tree's scientific name is *Quercus alba* (or *Q. alba* after the first time the full name is used). The tree belongs to the genus *Quercus*, which includes all oaks. The second part of the name, *alba,* refers only to the white oak species.

Linneaus named hundreds of species. Other scientists quickly adopted his highly flexible system to name thousands more. The Linnean system appeared at a time when European naturalists were exploring the rest of the world, finding thousands of new plants and animals. This flood of discoveries was overwhelming at times, but Linnaean taxonomy helped scientists identify and organize their finds for systematic study.

MODERN TAXONOMY

Biologists still use the system of scientific naming that Linnaeus developed (anyone who discovers a new species of plant or animal can choose its scientific name, which must be in Latin). Other aspects of taxonomy, though, have changed since Linnaeus's time.

As biologists have learned more about living things, they have added new levels to taxonomy to reflect their growing understanding of the similarities and differences among organisms. An organism's full classification might now include the following taxonomic levels: kingdom, subkingdom, division (for plants and fungi) or phylum (for animals), subdivision or subphylum, superclass, class, subclass, infraclass, order, superfamily,

Classifying the Prairie Lupine

Scientists are currently debating which of several different systems are best for classifying the hundreds of thousands of species that make up the plant kingdom. Still, Linnaean taxonomy, the oldest of these systems, remains the most widely used. Linnaean taxonomy is a series of levels or categories, with each level including all of the categories below it. Here are the main taxonomic levels used today:

Kingdom
Division   (for plants and fungi) or Phylum (for animals)

            Subdivision or Subphylum

Class
Order

        Suborder
        Infraorder
        Superfamily

Family
Genus
Species

The prairie lupine (*Lupinus lepidus*), a North American wildflower, is classified this way in the Linnaean system:

Kingdom   Plantae (plants)
Division   Magnoliophyta (flowering plants)
Class   Magnoliopsida (dicotyledons— plants with two seed leaves)
Subclass   Rosidae (many-petaled plants; may have multiple stamens)
Family   Fabaceae (irregular flowers; fruit is a legume such as a
            bean or pea)
Subfamily Papilionoideae (largest of three subfamilies; only subfamily well
            represented outside the tropics)
Genus   *Lupinus* (all lupines)
Species   *lepidus* (the prairie lupine)

family, genus, species, and subspecies or variety. Most discussions of plants, however, rely on the basic taxonomic levels of division, class, order, and family.

Another change concerns the kinds of information that scientists use to classify organisms. The earliest naturalists used obvious physical features, such as the differences between reptiles and mammals, to divide organisms into general groups. By the time of Ray and Linnaeus, naturalists could study specimens in more detail. Aided by new tools such as the microscope, they explored the inner structures of plants and animals. For a long time after Linnaeus, classification was based mainly on details of

Flowering plants take an enormous variety of forms, from bamboo (left), a member of the grass family that typically flourishes in moist climates, to the desert-loving cactus (right). This rare black-spined lace cactus, an endangered subspecies of a common species, grows only around the town of Alice, Texas.

anatomy, or physical structure, although scientists also looked at how an organism reproduced and how and where it lived.

Biologists can now peer more deeply into an organism's inner workings than Aristotle or Linnaeus ever dreamed possible. They can look inside its individual cells and study the arrangement of DNA that makes up its genetic blueprint. Genetic information is key to modern classification because DNA is more than an organism's blueprint—it also contains clues about how closely that organism is related to other species and how long ago those species separated during the process of evolution.

There is no single, final taxonomy on which all scientists agree. Experts sometimes disagree on certain points. They may often debate whether two organisms belong to the same species or to different species, or whether an organism represents a new species. Even at the highest level of classification, scientists hold differing views. A few divide life into as many as thirteen kingdoms. Most scientists, though, use systems of classification that have five to eight kingdoms: plants, animals, fungi, and two to five kingdoms of microscopic organisms such as bacteria, amoebas, and algae.

In recent years, a few biologists have suggested abandoning Linnaean taxonomy and scientific naming. The Linnaean system, they rightly point out, is a patchwork of old and new ideas. It doesn't clearly reflect the latest knowledge about evolutionary connections among organisms living and extinct. These taxonomists call for a new system based entirely on evolutionary relationships. None of the proposed new systems has yet won universal acceptance. Scientists continue to use the two main features of Linnaean taxonomy: the hierarchy of categories and the two-part scientific name. However, plant and animal classifications now change often as scientists apply new evolutionary insights to taxonomy. Such insights have caused botanists to move plants into different categories and even to rearrange the categories themselves. Genetic research continues to bring changes to the centuries-old science of classifying living things.

PLANT KINGDOM

Scientists arrange living things into patterns to highlight the
This is one of several classifications

KINGDOMS

Animals

Plants

Fungi
(Fungi,
Lichens)

DIVISIONS

Bryophytes
(Mosses)

Polytrichum moss

Sphenophytes
(Horsetails)

Field horsetail

Pterophytes
(Ferns)

Brackenfern

Psilophytes
(Whisk Ferns)

Whisk fern

Lycopodophytes
(Club Mosses)

Stiff club moss

14

FAMILY TREE

connections and differences among the many forms of life.
scientists have developed for the plant kingdom.

Monerans
(Bacteria)

Protoctists
(Algae, Slimemolds, Protozoa)

Cycadophytes
(Cycads)

Sago palm

Coniferophytes
(Conifers)

Black spruce

Gnetophytes
(Gnetums, Ephedras,
Welwitschias)

Green Mormon tea

Ginkgophytes
(Ginkgos)

Ginkgo

Magnoliophytes
(Angiosperms or
Flowering Plants)

Lily of the valley

Blazing red bigtooth maples paint Texas's Gaudalupe Mountains with autumn colors. Maples are deciduous trees, which means that they shed their leaves for winter—often after the leaves turn a variety of colors. The spiky plant in the foreground is a sotol, a drought-resistant plant whose long leaves are edged with spines.

The Flowering of The World

Botanists don't yet know how many different species of plants exist on earth—their estimates range from 260,000 to 400,000. They think, however, that flowering plant species outnumber other kinds of plants by a very large margin. At least 90 percent of the plant species on earth are angiosperms. Surprisingly, flowering plants are not only the most abundant form of plant life but also the youngest in geological time. Other kinds of plants have existed far longer than angiosperms, but the remarkably successful angiosperms now vastly outnumber them. Scientists are uncovering new evidence about when the first flowering plants evolved from earlier forms of plant life. They are also filling in the story of how those primitive angiosperms developed into the hundreds of thousands of species of flowering plants in the world today.

THE EVOLUTION OF PLANTS

The oldest known fossils of living things date from around 3.5 to 3.7 billion years ago. They are traces of microbes, tiny one-celled organisms thought to be the ancestors of all life. These early life forms inhabited oceans and resembled cyanobacteria, or blue-green algae, which are microorganisms that still exist today.

For several billion years, all life on earth consisted of simple, ocean-dwelling microorganisms, each of which had a single cell or a few simple cells. These microorganisms evolved into a variety of forms. Some contained the chemical chlorophyll, which is vital to photosynthesis, the process that allows certain living cells to manufacture food from water, sunlight, and the atmospheric gas carbon dioxide. Researchers believe that by 3.3 million years ago, photosynthesis was taking place in shallow ocean waters.

The beginning of photosynthesis was a milestone in the history of life on earth. Living things that photosynthesize take in carbon dioxide and give off oxygen. Over long ages, photosynthesis by the growing population of single-celled, chlorophyll-containing microorganisms in the world's oceans changed the earth's atmosphere, lowering the amount of carbon dioxide it contained and raising the amount of oxygen. Photosynthesis created a world in which oxygen-breathing life forms could evolve.

Life remained microscopic but grew more complex. Scientists believe that after about 2.7 billion years ago new kinds of organisms, complex cells called eukaryotes, appeared. A eukaryote is a cell that contains a distinct nucleus, an internal structure separated from the rest of the cell by a membrane. The oldest known fossil traces of eukaryotic organisms date from 2.1 billion years ago and are of single-celled green algae.

By 800 million years ago, more complex forms of green algae had evolved into multicelled organisms, in which many cells joined together in strands or ribbons. These seaweeds were plantlike organisms, although most scientists do not view algae as part of the plant kingdom. (Both single-celled and multicelled algae are usually placed in the kingdom Protoctista, which includes a variety of microorganisms called protoctists or protozoans. Some protoctists have plant characteristics, and some have animal characteristics.) A variety of multicelled algae and other small

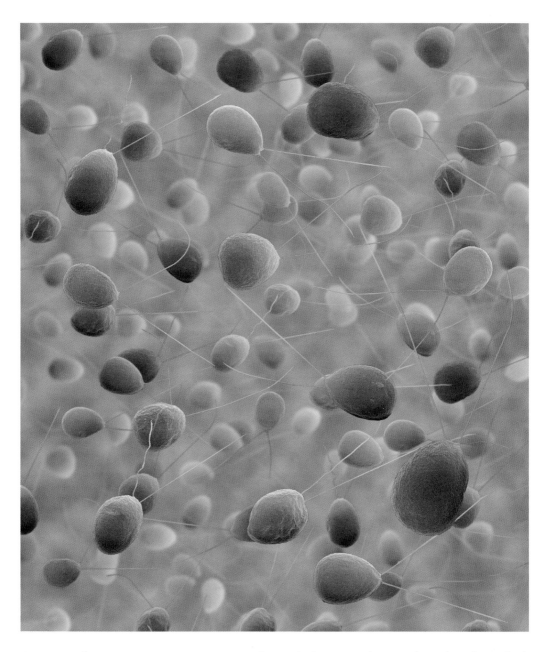

A scanning electron microscope gives scientists a close-up look at green algae, similar to those that evolved more than two billion years ago. Like those earliest photosynthesizing organisms, these green algae contain chlorophyll, a chemical that lets them produce energy from sunlight and gives them their green color.

plants existed in the ocean by 540 million years ago. So did the earliest animals, also evolved from microorganisms. Because of the growing abundance and diversity of these ancestral life forms, scientists have given the name Paleozoic ("ancient life") Era to the span of time between 570 and 245 million years ago.

Another major milestone in the history of life occurred early in the Paleozoic Era, when life left the sea and colonized the world's land masses. The first terrestrial, or land-dwelling, organisms were plants.

Marine plants were surrounded and supported by water. Water carried nutrients to each plant cell and carried the plants' gametes, or reproductive cells, to each other. Life on dry land, exposed to the air, would require some changes. Fossil evidence suggests that around 470 million years ago, groups of specialized cells began to evolve within some marine plants. These cells performed new functions: they carried water and nutrients within the plants and provided physical support. In addition, new types of reproductive cells evolved, with chemical substances in the cell walls that protected the cells from damage caused by drying out or by ultraviolent light in the atmosphere. Some plant cells also began to develop a cuticle, a waxy surface layer to protect against water loss and ultraviolet damage. Some paleobotanists, scientists who specialize in ancient plant life, think that these features evolved in green algae that lived in shallow coastal waters or tide pools, places that sometimes dried out. After adapting to environments that were occasionally dry, plants could colonize dry land. The first fossils of algae-like terrestrial plants are about 430 million years old. Plants may have existed on land before that time, but no earlier fossils have been found.

The earliest land plants evolved into new forms that fully fit the scientific definition of plants: multicelled, eukaryotic organisms that manufacture their own food through photosynthesis. First to develop were a group of plants that botanists call bryophytes—the liverworts, hornworts, and mosses. Descendants of these ancient bryophytes still exist today. By 408 million years ago, the bryophytes had given rise to a new group, the vascular plants. Unlike algae and bryophytes, vascular plants have a kind of

One of the oldest known vascular land plants is *Cooksonia pertoni*; this fossil, found in Great Britain, is 410 million years old. The four species of *Cooksonia* are named for Australian botanist Isabel C. Cookson, a collector and researcher of plant fossils.

circulatory system: an internal structure of specialized, hollow cells through which food, water, and minerals move from one part of the plant to another. The earliest vascular plants were pteridophytes. Surviving members of this group include ferns and horsetails.

At first all plants were small, about 4 inches (10 centimeters) tall at most. But while non-vascular land plants remained small, vascular plants evolved into larger and more varied forms. Features such as roots, wood, bark, and leaves began to evolve. Many species of ferns and horsetails grew to heights of 33 feet (10 meters). Some were two or three times taller. They formed the world's first forests.

Mosses and ferns reproduce by scattering tiny fertilized eggs called spores. By 350 million years ago, a new type of plant reproduction had evolved, and the first seed-bearing plants appeared. The fertilized egg of a seed-bearing plant is called an embryo. Unlike a spore, it is surrounded by nutrients and enclosed in a protective shell or coating. Together the embryo, its food supply, and its coating form a seed.

Seed-bearing plants have a big advantage over the more ancient forms of plant life. Seeds are better than spores at surviving extreme heat, cold,

A 225-million-year-old fossilized cycad leaf from Arizona. Cycads are often mistakenly called palms, which they resemble in some ways, but they are not flowering plants like palms.

TIMELINE OF PLANT EVOLUTION

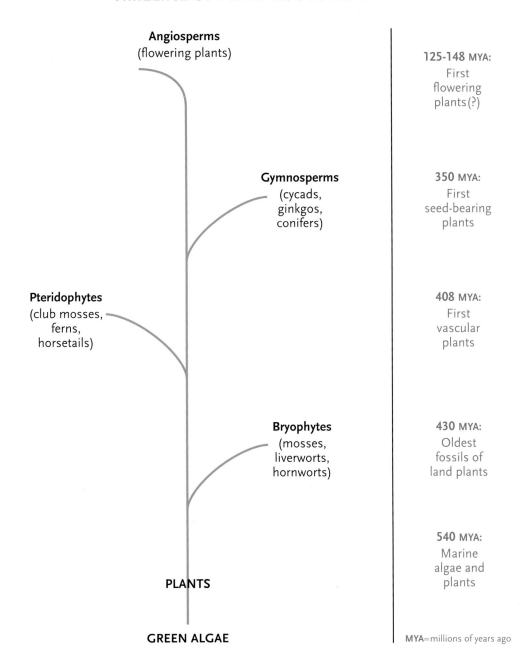

Angiosperms
(flowering plants)

125-148 MYA:
First
flowering
plants(?)

Gymnosperms
(cycads,
ginkgos,
conifers)

350 MYA:
First
seed-bearing
plants

Pteridophytes
(club mosses,
ferns,
horsetails)

408 MYA:
First
vascular
plants

Bryophytes
(mosses,
liverworts,
hornworts)

430 MYA:
Oldest
fossils of
land plants

540 MYA:
Marine
algae and
plants

PLANTS

GREEN ALGAE

MYA=millions of years ago

or dryness. They can wait until conditions are right before they germinate, or start growing. This advantage let seed-bearing plants spread into a wide range of terrestrial environments, from tropical to arctic, completing the colonization of land by the plant kingdom. New types of seed-bearing trees evolved between 290 and 206 million years ago. The first to appear were many kinds of cycads and ginkgos. Most have become extinct, but a few cycads and one ginkgo species still exist. Next to evolve were the conifers, which generally bear their seeds in cone-shaped clusters. Among the conifers that survive today are pines, spruces, cedars, firs, junipers, redwoods, and cypresses.

From coastlines slick with algae to mossy swamplands to vast expanses of ginkgo, cycad, and conifer forests, plants had turned the world green. The next stage in plant evolution would fill it with colorful, fragrant blooms.

THE ANGIOSPERMS APPEAR

Cycads, ginkgos, and conifers are all gymnosperms, a name that comes from the Greek words for "naked seed." The next group of plants to evolve was the flowering plants or angiosperms, whose name comes from words meaning "enclosed seed." Angiosperms' defining feature is that their seeds develop within chambers called carpels, which contain the ovaries or female reproductive parts of flowers. Paleobotanists think that carpels evolved from leaves. Over time, certain leaves grew more and more tightly folded until they enclosed the plants' ovules, or seeds, in protective chambers. Once the seeds have ripened, the carpels become fruits. Angiosperms are the only plants that produce flowers and fruits.

When did the first angiosperms appear? That question has long perplexed scientists. Charles Darwin, who founded evolutionary science when he published *On the Origin of Species* in 1859, called the origin of angiosperms an "abominable mystery." Darwin was frustrated because flowering plants seemed to have appeared on earth suddenly. The fossils known in his day offered no clues as to how or when angiosperms might have evolved from gymnosperms. Since Darwin's time, however, scientists have learned more about the first flowering plants. Some of the most exciting discoveries have occurred in recent years.

Fossil finds in the middle of the twentieth century led paleobotanists to think that the earliest angiosperms were similar to modern magnolias. That idea grew stronger later in the century, when genetic science emerged as a new form of biological research. Experts examined the DNA of living angiosperms, looking for the oldest species or group now in existence. They hoped that by tracing shared and inherited traits they could

This blossoming magnolia tree belongs to one of the more ancient surviving families of flowering plants. Magnolias—which exist in more than eighty species—are native to regions ranging from Japan and the Himalayas to Ontario and the American South.

Amborella trichopoda, a small shrub found in the wild only on one Pacific island, has primitive features—for example, it lacks vessels to carry water from the soil into its leaves. According to recent studies of plant DNA, *A. trichopoda* is the oldest surviving flowering plant. All of its close relatives are extinct.

build a family tree for flowering plants. This approach revealed that a group of small, magnolia-like woody plants called the Amborellaceae has an ancient heritage. Most members of this group are extinct, but a single species, *Amborella trichopoda,* survives on the South Pacific island of New Caledonia. Considered a living fossil, it is descended from ancestors that flourished more than 120 million years ago.

Amborella trichopoda may be the most ancient flowering plant alive today, but that does not mean that it was the first to evolve. A better candidate for the ancestral angiosperm emerged from a limestone bed in China in 1998. It was a partial fossil of a small flowering plant belonging to a species new to science. A second fossil was found four years later, complete with roots, leaves, and reproductive organs, including seeds encased in an immature fruit. Named *Archaefructus sinensis* ("ancient fruit from China"), the plant has some magnolia-like characteristics but differs from the woody Amborellaceae. Because fossils of fish were found among the plant's branches, scientists think that *A. sinensis* probably grew in shallow pools, raising its reproductive organs above the water's surface, as water lilies do today. They estimate that it lived at least 125 million years ago, and possibly as early as 148 million years ago. It is the oldest flowering plant known with certainty from fossil evidence—for now.

Scientists ever since Charles Darwin in the nineteenth century have wondered when the first flowering plants evolved. This fossil of *Archaefructus liaoningensis,* along with fossils of its relative, *A. sinensis,* are evidence of the oldest angiosperms known so far—between 125 and 148 million years old. Found in China, they probably grew in shallow water.

In the early twenty-first century, researchers at California's Stanford University suggested that the evolution of flowering plants might have begun with the gigantopterids, a group of long-extinct seed-bearing plants that lived between 290 and 245 million years ago. According to the Stanford scientists, some gigantopterid fossils contain traces of a chemical called oleanane. Many modern angiosperms produce oleanane, but no gymnosperms are known to make it. The Stanford group therefore believes that gigantopterids were not gymnosperms but rather early relatives of the angiosperms. Not all botanists accept an argument based on chemistry, however. Many want clearer fossil evidence of angiosperm anatomy before pushing the origin of flowering plants so far into the past.

FLOWERING PLANTS TODAY

Once they had originated, flowering plants quickly evolved into a dizzying array that scientists would later group into thousands of orders, families, genera, and species. Botanists are still grappling with the challenge of classifying the world's most numerous and varied form of plant life. Several different classification schemes for plants are now in use. Articles in scientific journals frequently propose changes to those schemes or offer whole new systems.

Traditionally, botanists divided flowering plants into two groups based on whether a germinating seed produces one or two cotyledons, which are the first leaves to appear when a seed sprouts. Monocotyledons, or monocots, produce one seed leaf. The leaves of monocots have parallel veins.

Pineapples originated in the tropical and subtropical Americas. In the seventeenth century, the fruit of the pineapple was so rare and costly in Europe that an official portrait of King Charles II of England shows him with one, a symbol of wealth and status. Today pineapples are grown commercially in many parts of the world.

Rhododendrons, grown in many cool climates as decorative plants and prized for their showy spring blooms, are dicotyledons, or dicots, one of the two subclasses of flowering plants. Its leaves have veins that branch out from a central vein or node, a trait found in dicots. Monocot leaves have parallel veins.

Almost all monocots are herbaceous, lacking in woody tissue. (Lilies, orchids, grasses, and palm trees are examples of monocots.) Dicotyledons, or dicots, produce two seed leaves. Their leaves have branching veins, and the plants may be either woody or herbaceous. Botanist Arthur Cronquist presented a plant taxonomy that uses this traditional division in his 1992 book *An Integrated System of Classification of Flowering Plants.* In Cronquist's system, flowering plants form a division called Magnoliophyta. The division has two classes: Liliopsidae (monocots) and Magnoliopsidae (dicots).

A New Use, a New Name

Scientists change a plant's name or classification when they gain new knowledge about its relationship to other plants. Sometimes that knowledge has important practical uses, as in the case of a tree called the Moreton Bay chestnut.

For a long time the Moreton Bay chestnut, or *Castanospermum australe,* was the only species in the genus *Castanospermum.* In the 1990s researchers discovered that castanospermine, a chemical that the tree produces, can be used to make drugs that help in the treatment of AIDS. Unfortunately, Moreton Bay chestnut trees are found only in one place— eastern Australia—and they do not produce much castanospermine. Researchers looked for the closest relatives of the Moreton Bay chestnut. These turned out to be American trees of the genus *Alyxa.* When the American trees proved to contain castanospermine, their scientific classification was changed. All of them were moved into the *Castanospermum* genus along with the Moreton Bay chestnut. With no member species remaining, the *Alyxa* genus was eliminated, or, as taxonomists say, "sunk."

The five subclasses of Liliopsidae contain two to six orders each. The six subclasses of Magnoliopsidae contain three to eighteen orders each. Cronquist's system is widely used. So is another very similar classification that groups all vascular plants together in the Tracheophyta division of the plant kingdom. Within that divison, flowering plants form the class Anthopsidae, with subclasses of monocots and dicots.

Recently, some botanists have developed systems of classification that focus on plants' evolutionary history. Called cladistic or phylogenetic classification, this approach groups together only plants that are known to share a common ancestor. The Angiosperm Phylogeny Group (APG), made up of scientists from many institutions in several countries, has developed a classification using cladistics. The APG recognizes the species, genus, family, and order levels of traditional taxonomy but doesn't always place families and orders in higher groups. The APG regards the class and division levels of taxonomy as informal, not based on well-established evolutionary history. The cladistic approach has also challenged the traditional division of flowering plants into monocots and dicots. Some botanists now recognize three broad groups: monocots, eudicots (most dicots), and a much smaller group called magnoliids (the remaining dicots).

Changes occur constantly in the naming and classifying of flowering plants. The structure of flowering plants, though, has been well known for many years. An anatomical sketch of a flowering plant in a modern botany textbook would look quite familiar to Linnaeus and Darwin.

Catkins are dangling clusters of small flowers on many kinds of trees, including hazels, birches, and oaks. These catkins are the male flowers of an oak tree. They bear pollen that the wind will carry to female flowers, on the same tree or another. Catkins also provide food for some species of birds and small animals.

Anatomy of an Angiosperm

One of the chief functions of flowering plants and other living things is reproducing themselves. A botanist interested in plant reproduction might even say that an oak tree is just an acorn's way of making another acorn. But in order to reproduce, plants must survive and nourish themselves. Three of the four main parts of an angiosperm's structure provide support and nourishment. These are the roots, stems, and leaves, sometimes called the vegetative organs. The fourth part is the reproductive organ, the flower, which produces fruits and seeds. People love flowers for their graceful shapes, brilliant colors, and appealing scents. All of these are features that evolved to help angiosperms' sexual organs do their job more efficiently—to attract pollinators.

ROOTS

Roots are the base of a flowering plant. The roots of free-floating plants, such as duckweed, dangle into the water. Those of some plants, including certain kinds of climbing vines, fasten themselves to the stems or branches

33

MAIN PARTS OF A PLANT

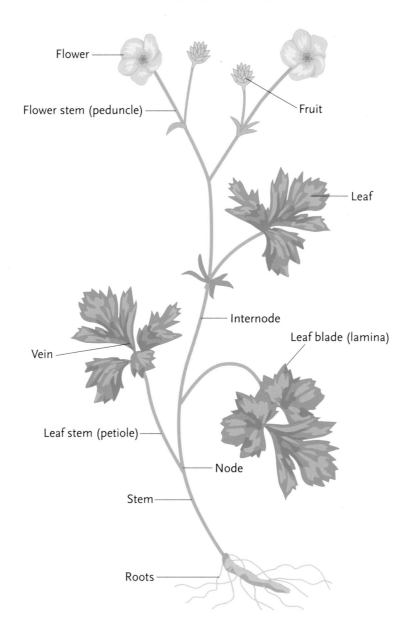

Flower

Flower stem (peduncle)

Fruit

Leaf

Internode

Leaf blade (lamina)

Vein

Leaf stem (petiole)

Node

Stem

Roots

of other plants. Most angiosperm roots, however, are underground. As soon as a seed germinates, it sends out a primary root that grows downward through the soil. Later, secondary or lateral roots branch out from the primary root. Smaller rootlets may grow out from both primary and lateral roots. The root systems of mature plants form two kinds of structures. Fibrous structures have many roots of about the same size, spread equally in all directions. In taproot structures, the primary root remains much larger than the rest and grows straight down.

Roots perform several functions. Like anchors, they hold plants in place. Roots also absorb two things that plants need from soil: water and minerals. Trees and many other plants have mycorrhizae, which are fungi attached to roots. The fungi help the plants absorb water and nutrients; the plants provide food for the fungi. Some roots serve a third purpose as well. They store food for the plants—and, often, for animals and people who dig them up to

Grass has a fibrous root structure, with many roots of about the same size.

Carrots have a taproot structure, with a primary downward-pointing root. In the case of carrots, the crunchy yellow-orange cone that we call a vegetable is actually the taproot itself.

eat. Carrots, sweet potatoes, and cassava are three of the many nutritious roots.

Roots contain vascular tissue, also found in stems and leaves. Vascular tissue is made of specialized cells that form two types of hollow tubes inside the plants. Xylem carries water and minerals from the roots into the stem and leaves. Phloem carries food manufactured by photosynthesis in the leaves to the stem and the roots. The transport system of xylem and phloem runs through all vascular plants, not just angiosperms.

STEMS

The stem, along with the roots, is a plant's primary support structure. Most stems grow upright above the ground, although some grow along the ground or beneath its surface. There are two main kinds of stems, woody and herbaceous.

Woody stems are stiff because their outer layers contain large amounts of tough xylem. The outer surface of a woody stem is usually some shade of brown or gray and may be either smooth or rough. Gases enter and leave the stem through thousands of tiny holes or pores called lenticels. Woody stems are found on trees and bushes. Such stems can reach great sizes and last for many years.

Herbaceous stems, also called nonwoody stems, are green and soft. They contain much less xylem than woody stems. In general, herbaceous plants are smaller than woody plants and have shorter lives. Many of them live for just one year. When herbaceous plants live longer than a year in places where frosts occur, their stems and other aboveground parts often die away during the winter, to regrow in the spring.

Like roots, stems serve several purposes. They are the framework that supports and displays the plant's leaves, where food is made, and its flowers, where reproduction takes

European explorers named this tropical angiosperm the bird of paradise plant because its dramatic shape reminded them of a rare and striking tropical bird.

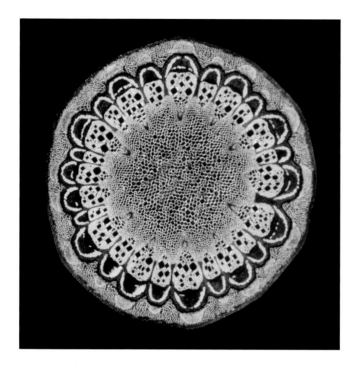

Lacier than the most elaborate snowflake, the cross-section of this plant's stem reveals the many hollow tubes or vessels through which water and liquid nutrients travel. Plants whose tissue contains such vessels are called vascular plants.

place. Stems are also part of the plant's transport system, with vascular tissues that carry water, minerals, and food between roots and leaves. Bundles of xylem and phloem cells run through herbaceous stems. Woody plants have a layer of phloem inside their bark. Inside that is a layer of xylem.

LEAVES

Flowering plants sprout leaves in many sizes and types, from a cactus's stiff, pointed needles to the 65-foot-long, 8-foot-broad (32-meter-long, 2.4-meter-broad) fronds of the raffia palm. Although leaves occur in various shades of reddish brown and yellow, most are green.

A leaf has two main parts, the petiole and the lamina. The petiole is the stalk that attaches the leaf to the stem. The lamina is the flat body of the leaf. Small tubes called veins run through each leaf. Vascular tissues in these veins and in the petiole carry water and nutrients into and out of the leaves. The surface of each leaf also has many tiny pores called stomata, through which gases enter and leave.

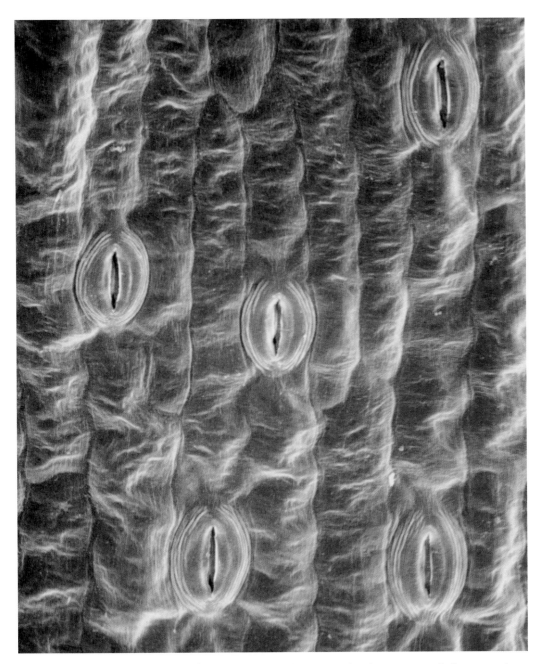

The surface of a leaf, magnified 200 times, has rows of cells dotted with openings called stomata, the pores through which gases enter and leave the plant.

TYPES OF LEAVES

Simple Leaves

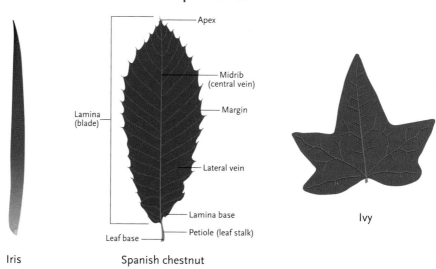

Iris

Spanish chestnut

Ivy

Compound Leaves

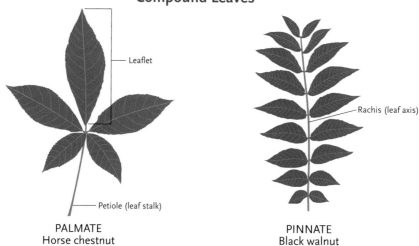

PALMATE
Horse chestnut

PINNATE
Black walnut

Leaves are either simple or compound. A simple leaf has a single petiole, or stalk, and a single lamina, the blade or body of the leaf. A compound leaf has multiple blades. There are two types of compound leaves, palmate and pinnate. In palmate leaves, all of the blades radiate from the tip of the petiole. In pinnate leaves, the petiole becomes a central axis called a rachis, which runs the length of the leaf, and small separate blades are attached to it by their own stalks.

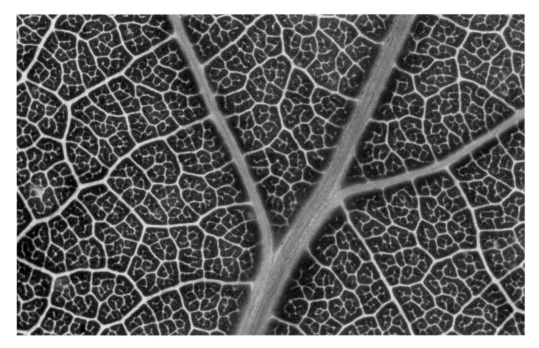

A lot goes on in a leaf. The green color is a sign of chlorophyll, the key agent in photosynthesis, by which cells produce food for the plant. The midrib, or central vein, is both a structural support for the leaf and the largest of the network of veins that transport liquids. Smaller veins appear white.

There are two basic types of leaves, simple and compound. A simple leaf may be round, or oval, or long and slender like a grass leaf. Or, like a maple or oak leaf, it may have several sections called lobes, like fingers spreading out from the palm of a hand. However it is shaped, though, every simple leaf has one petiole and one lamina. In a compound leaf, the petiole bears multiple leaf blades, which are known as leaflets. Some compound leaves have leaflets arranged in rows on either side of the central stalk. This is called a pinnate leaf structure. Others have a palmate leaf structure, with leaflets branching out from the tip of the petiole.

Whatever their size or shape, leaves are the food factories of plants. Inside them photosynthesis takes place, combining energy from the sun with water and minerals to form the food that fuels the plant's growth and reproduction.

FLOWERS

People have long used flowers as symbols of beauty and love—for example, think of the role that bouquets traditionally play in weddings. Flowers also represent life and rebirth, because they bloom anew after each winter. Flowers may have held these symbolic meanings for the Neandertal people, early humans who lived in Europe and western Asia tens of thousands of years ago. Some Neandertal graves contain traces of flowers that must have been placed there, perhaps as tokens of affection, when the dead were buried. More recently, the English poet William Blake wrote about seeing "heaven in a wild flower."

By Blake's time, however, scientists had recognized that flowers are more than lovely ornaments. They are the angiosperms' organs of reproduction. Although there are exceptions, a flower is typically both male and female. Each contains structures that produce male and female gametes,

PARTS OF A FLOWER

Carpel
- Stigma
- Style
- Ovary

Anther
Filament
Stamen

Pollen

Petal (corolla)

Ovule

Sepal (calyx)

Receptacle

The flower of the yellow bee orchid has evolved to resemble a bee feeding on a yellow-green flower. Some botanists think that this adaptation tricks bees into landing on the orchid, which does not produce nectar to attract them. If a bee sees what it thinks is another bee eating, goes the theory, then it will try to eat there, too. When the bee lands on the flower, it will collect pollen, which it will later carry to another flower. But bee orchids do not count on bees to do all their pollination; their pollen is also carried by the wind.

The spring flowers of the red maple tree have clusters of stamens, each topped by a pollen-producing anther.

the cells that unite in sexual reproduction. Some species, however, bear separate male and female flowers, either on the same plant or on different plants. Even more than leaves, flowers are enormously varied in size, shape, and color. There is variety in their structures, too, but almost all flowers have four main sections: calyx, corolla, stamens, and carpels.

The calyx shields the flower's inner parts while it is developing. Then, when the flower opens and matures, the calyx remains next to the receptacle, the cuplike structure that attaches the flower to its stalk. On dicots, the calyx usually consists of small, green outer petals called sepals. Inside the calyx is the corolla, the ring of flower petals. The corolla gives each flower its distinctive appearance, from the tiny white blossoms of the strawberry plant to the lushest of red roses. The sepals and petals of monocots usually look alike, with no visible difference between the calyx and the corolla.

Stamens are the flower's male sex organs. Most flowers have more than one stamen. A stamen consists of a stalk called a filament, topped by a structure called an anther, which produces pollen that contains the plant's male gametes, or sperm. The plant's female sex organs are called carpels (some sources call them pistils). Depending upon the species, a flower may have one carpel or many. At the top of each carpel is a flat surface called a stigma. A tube called a style connects the stigma with the ovary, a chamber at the base of the carpel. The ovary contains one or more ovules, which produce the plant's female gametes, or eggs.

The passionflower's blossom has both male and female sex organs. The stamens, which are topped with rounded anthers, are the source of male sex cells. The carpels or pistils, with flat tops called stigmas, lead to chambers holding female sex cells.

Flowers are grouped on their stalks in many different ways. In some species, each stalk bears a single flower. Tiger lilies and roses are examples of single flowerheads. Lily-of-the-valley illustrates a different arrangement, in which individual flowers branch off from the same main stalk. Foxglove flowers are also arranged along a main stalk. They are also an example of the kind of flower created when the individual petals are joined together to form a single tubelike petal.

In the foxglove flower, the petals have merged to form a single petal that is something like a tube. The shape of the flower inspired the plant's folk names, which include fairy caps (or thimbles), witch's gloves, dead men's bells, and bloody fingers.

The sunflower is an inflorescence—many flowers that look like one large one. Each of the spikes in the center is a small flower.

Many species of plants produce multiple flowerheads called inflorescences, in which each stalk bears many small flowers. For example, each tiny yellow spike on a dandelion stalk is an individual flower. And although a sunflower appears to be a single large flower, is really an inflorescence of multiple flowers. Each of the dark-brown spikes in the center of a sunflower is a floret, or small flower. The surrounding yellow petals are specialized florets that don't produce sex cells. In the world of angiosperms, what looks like a flower may be a hundred or even a thousand flowers.

SPECIAL ADAPTATIONS

Flowering plants live in a wide range of environments, including very dry or wet places and places with poor soil or even no soil at all. They have evolved a variety of special adaptations that allow them to survive and even flourish in these environments.

Angiosperms that live in deserts and other places with very little water are called xerophytes. Many xerophytes have unusually thick cuticles, the waterproof waxy coatings that lock moisture into leaves and stems while preventing damage from strong sunlight. Xerophytes often have very small leaves, which reduces the surface area from which water can evaporate into the air. The leaves of cacti, for example, have become extremely narrow and tough—they are needles or spines. Cacti are succulents, xerophytes that have evolved thick tissues to absorb and store water like sponges. Many other kinds of xerophytes are also succulents, storing moisture in their roots, stems, or leaves.

Cacti are xerophytes, plants adapted to live in dry conditions. They have thick tissues to store water and a waxy coating that locks in moisture and protects the plant tissues from strong sunlight. To reduce the surface area that could lose moisture to the air, the leaves of cacti have evolved into narrow needles.

Angiosperms that live in water have evolved a different set of adaptations. They are partly or entirely supported by water, so their roots, stems, and leaves need little of the sturdy supportive tissue that holds up land plants. Instead, the roots, stems, and leaves of water plants contain hollow spaces filled with air. These chambers add buoyancy, helping the plants float. The underwater parts of these plants lack a cuticle so that the plants can absorb nutrients and gases directly from the water.

Plants need certain minerals from the soil. In the moist environments called bogs, however, the soil tends to lack nitrates and other necessary minerals. Some plants have adapted to bog life by getting the minerals they need from other sources—from insects and small animals. These are the carnivorous, or meat-eating, plants. Flytraps, pitcher plants, sundews, butterworts, and bladderworts have evolved different mechanisms for luring and trapping animal prey that ranges in size from gnats to frogs and even

Glistening drops of moisture inside the wells of these pitcher plants lure insects to take a drink. The drops turn out to be sticky, and the insects are trapped. Dissolved and digested, the unlucky insects will provide much-needed mineral nutrients to the carnivorous—meat-eating—plants.

Epiphytic orchids in Hawaii. Epiphytes, sometimes called "air plants," do not root themselves in soil or float in water. Instead, they attach themselves to other plants. The epiphytes don't harm the host plants—they simply use them as supports and produce their own food through photosynthesis.

small rats. The plants produce chemicals called enzymes that dissolve or digest the prey so that the plants can absorb the mineral nutrients contained in the prey's tissues.

Instead of growing in soil or water, some plants grow on other plants. Epiphytes such as some orchids and bromeliads fasten themselves to the stems or branches of host plants, usually trees. They absorb minerals from organic material that has built up on the tree bark. They get water from the air or collect pools of rainwater among their leaves. Like most other plants, epiphytes create food through photosynthesis. Some plants that live on other plants, however, do not perform their own photosynthesis. Instead, they send their roots into the host plants to absorb food that the hosts have manufactured photosynthetically. Such plants are called parasites. Broomrape and dodder are fairly common parasites. One of the rarest parasites is *Rafflesia arnoldii*, which grows in tropical Southeast

Rafflesia arnoldii, a parasitic plant found only on the island of Sumatra, produces the world's largest flower. One of several plants to earn the nickname "corpse plant" or "corpse flower," *Rafflesia* produces what one traveler in 1928 called "a penetrating smell more repulsive than any buffalo carcass in an advanced state of decomposition."

Asia. It produces the world's largest flower, as much as 3 feet (1 meter) across. The strong stench of this flower has earned *R. arnoldii* the nickname "corpse plant." Mistletoe is an example of a partial parasite, a plant that both drains food from its hosts and performs photosynthesis within its own leaves.

Angiosperms have a dazzling range of shapes and colors, and they live in almost every habitat on earth. In spite of this great variety, though, all flowering plants share certain basic processes: the cycles of plant life.

Plants That Move

One way that plants differ from animals is that they don't move about. They are rooted to the spot where they grow from the soil (except for water plants such as the duckweed, which move through the action of the water).

Of course, plants do move. They grow, they send out branches and shoots, and sometimes they climb up trees, twine around fenceposts, and even choke each other. Such movements happen much too slowly for us to see them—except in time-lapse films, which speed up a week's, month's, or year's growth and show it in a matter of minutes. When the first time-lapse films of garden and forest plants aired on television in the 1970s, audiences were stunned to see flowers, vines, and trees writhe, struggle, and compete with one another for light. Ordinarily, though, these slow processes are invisible.

But a few plants move so quickly that we can see their motions. If you touch *Mimosa pudica*, a member

When *Mimosa pudica*, (left) is touched, its leaflets instantly snap shut (shown on right). *M. pudica* is one of several plants that have the ability to move quickly in response to certain stimuli.

of the pea family, its leaflets will snap shut and its branches will fold up next to its stem. The plant responds so strongly to touch that it is called the sensitive plant. In the same way, the leaves of some insect-eating plants close quickly on their captive prey.

For years evolutionist Charles Darwin was fascinated by the telegraph or semaphore plant, a small Asian shrub whose leaves twitch or move without any breeze. In *The Power of Movement in Plants* (1880), the last book Darwin published during his lifetime, he described the plant's movements, which he believed were meant "to shoot off the drops of water" that remained on the leaves after a heavy rainfall. Since Darwin's time scientists have learned how the telegraph plant moves. Its leaves contain special cells called motor cells that draw water in and pump it out. They grow larger as water enters them and smaller as it leaves them. The rapid movement of the water, together with pressure changes within the motor cells, makes the leaves twitch and jerk, earning it yet another nickname: the dancing plant.

Two wildflowers: yellow lady's slipper and red Indian paintbrush.

Life Cycles

The life of a flowering plant is made up of cycles that repeat themselves over and over. Water constantly enters plants and leaves them again in a process called the water cycle. The cycle of day and night determines when plants will be able to produce food. A plant's entire life is another cycle, one that may be as short as a few days or as long as hundreds of years. Through reproduction, the plant makes sure that the cycle of life will continue in the next generation of plants.

THE WATER CYCLE: OSMOSIS AND TRANSPIRATION

Water enters plants through a process called osmosis. Most of it enters through the roots, especially the fine root hairs. During osmosis, moisture from the soil seeps through the walls of cells in the roots, carrying dissolved minerals and other nutrients with it. The water then travels through the rest of the plant by way of the xylem cells in the vascular tissue.

How does water move from the roots all the way up to the highest leaves? Water is not pushed up from the roots—it is drawn up from the leaves. Each leaf constantly breathes gases into the air through its stomata, or tiny pores. The gases flow out through the stomata because the pressure inside the leaf cells is greater than the pressure of the surrounding air. One of the gases is water vapor. Through this process, called transpiration, plants shed water into the atmosphere. And just as sucking on a straw pulls the last drops of water from the bottom of a cup, the outward flow of water vapor and other gases creates a tension or pull on the liquid water within the plant. That water moves upward to fill the space that has been left empty by the transpired vapor. Transpiration can draw water up for hundreds of feet in tall trees. Together, osmosis and transpiration keep a new supply of water and nutrients moving through each plant.

THE FOOD CYCLE: PHOTOSYNTHESIS AND RESPIRATION

Animals must eat to live. They consume either plants or other animals that have eaten plants. But plants do not eat—they manufacture their own food internally (except for parasites, which steal the food their host plants make). Plants make food by combining water and the gas carbon dioxide in the sunlight-powered process known as photosynthesis.

Photosynthesis occurs inside special cells called chloroplasts, found in leaves and in herbaceous stems. Chloroplasts contain chlorophyll, a chemical compound that absorbs energy from sunlight and also gives plants their green color. The energy absorbed from sunlight becomes the fuel that powers a chemical reaction inside the chloroplasts. The two ingredients of the reaction are water, which enters the plant through the root system, and the gas carbon dioxide, which enters from the atmosphere through the stomata. The hydrogen and oxygen atoms of the water join with the carbon and oxygen atoms of the carbon dioxide to form glucose, a sugar made of carbon, hydrogen, and oxygen that is the plant's food. It travels through the plant in the phloem, providing energy for growth and reproduction.

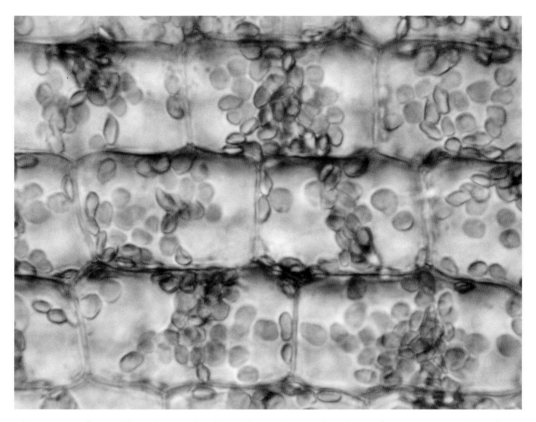

The green ovals are chloroplasts, cells where photosynthesis takes place. These tiny engines drive the food cycle of the entire Earth by converting sunlight into food for plants.

Respiration, which means "breathing," is another phase of the food cycle. Plants need oxygen to live, just as animals do. Green parts of plants make their own oxygen through photosynthesis. The extra oxygen they produce flows out through the stomata into the atmosphere—where it helps support other life forms. But photosynthesis cannot take place in the roots, because they do not receive light. Roots must get their oxygen from the soil, which is why it is very hard for plants to grow in soils that are low in oxygen.

PHOTOSYNTHESIS

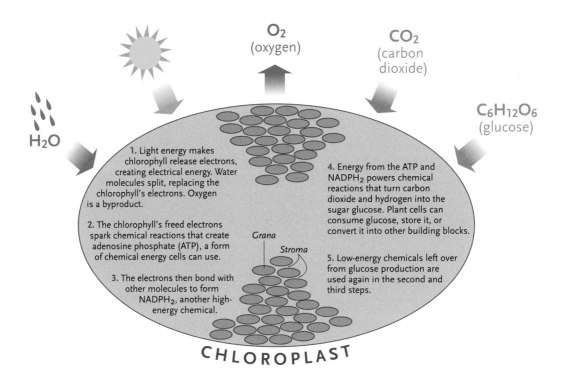

Photosynthesis takes place inside chloroplasts, tiny football-shaped bodies inside plant cells. They contain chlorophylls and other pigments that react with energy from sunlight. Steps 1 through 3 of photosynthesis take place in the grana, stacks of disk-shaped membranes packed inside the chloroplast. Scientists call steps 1 through 3 the light-dependent phase of photosynthesis because they require sunlight. Step 4 can occur with or without sunlight, so scientists call it the dark phase or light-independent phase of photosynthesis. Step 4 takes place in the stroma, a thick liquid that fills the chloroplast and surrounds the grana.

REPRODUCTION

Plants reproduce themselves in two ways. Sexual reproduction is the union of male and female gametes, the sex cells known as sperm and eggs, to create a seed. Genes from the two sex cells combine to create an offspring whose genetic makeup is different from both of them. Asexual or vegetative reproduction doesn't involve gametes. It takes place when some part of a plant, separated from the rest, grows into a complete new plant. A plant produced through asexual reproduction is a clone—its genetic makeup is identical to that of its parent plant.

Sexual reproduction begins with pollination. The anthers, the plant's male reproductive organs, produce tiny grains called pollen. Each pollen

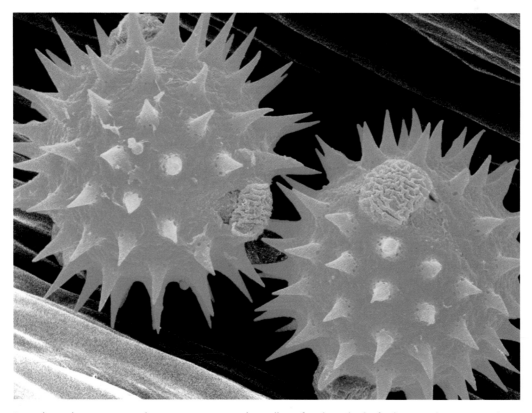

Seen through a scanning electron microscope, the pollen of a daisy looks frightening, but it is simply well-armed for its job. The spikes let the pollen grains, which contain the plant's male sex cells, stick to the hairs of insects that land on the plants. When the insects move on to other flowers, the pollen is transferred to new locations. If it happens to land on the female reproductive parts of a daisy, it will fertilize the egg to form a seed

grain contains two male sex cells. For pollination to occur, pollen must travel from the anthers to the stigma, the upper part of the plant's female reproductive organ. If the anther and stigma are on the same plant, the plant has self-pollinated. When anther from one plant lands on the stigma of another plant of the same species, the result is cross-pollination.

Pollen takes many routes from anthers to stigmas. It may fall or be knocked off the anther when the plant is jostled. Wind carries a great deal of pollen—as people with pollen allergies know all too well. Insects, birds, and animals also carry pollen, picking it up when they brush against anthers, later depositing it on stigmas. Creatures that carry pollen from plant to plant are called pollinators. Plants attract them with colorful flowers, sweet scents, and flavorful juices called nectars. Bees pollinate more flowers than any other creatures. Birds that live on nectar are

A rufous-breasted hermit hummingbird feasts on the nectar of a South American hibiscus flower. Some angiosperms have evolved to attract birds, not bees. Instead of scent, they lure pollinators with color, often some shade of red (bees do not see red, but birds do). They may have hanging flowers with long throats that make the nectar hard to reach without a long, specialized bill like that of the hummingbird or sunbird. In such cases, the flowers and birds have evolved on parallel tracks, biologists say, to meet each other's needs.

also important pollinators. Among these are hummingbirds in Central and South America and sunbirds in Africa and Asia.

Once pollen has landed on a stigma, the next step in reproduction is fertilization. Before the male and female gametes can unite, a male gamete from the pollen must reach the female gamete inside an ovule, at the opposite end of the pistil from the stigma. The pollen grain grows downward through the pistil, sending a tiny tube into the ovule. The two male sex cells from the pollen grain descend through the tube. One joins with the egg, or female gamete, to form the embryo of a new plant. The other, together with cells contained in the ovule, grows into a substance called endosperm, which will serve as food for the plant embryo. A coating called the seed coat forms around the embryo and the endosperm. Seed coat, endosperm,

Heavy fruits such as coconuts help spread seeds by rolling. Coconuts have also been known to remain fertile after floating for long distances or periods of time in the ocean. Botanists think that some subtropical and tropical islands were "colonized" by palms when coconuts washed up on their shores.

FROM SEED TO SEED

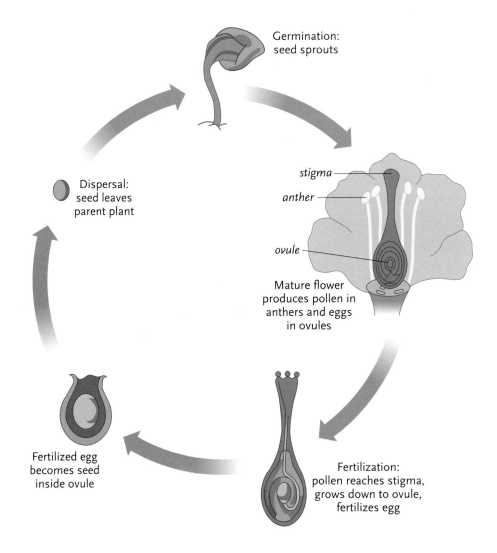

Germination: seed sprouts

stigma

anther

ovule

Mature flower produces pollen in anthers and eggs in ovules

Dispersal: seed leaves parent plant

Fertilized egg becomes seed inside ovule

Fertilization: pollen reaches stigma, grows down to ovule, fertilizes egg

and embryo together form a seed. When the seed has begun to form, the flower parts wither and fall away from the plant. The ovary—the chamber at the base of the pistil that contained the ovule—continues to hold the fertile seed (or seeds, if the ovary held more than one ovule) and may increase in size. It is the plant's fruit.

Fruits help to disperse, or spread, plant seeds. Some fruits, such as maple wings and dandelion fluff, have shapes that help seeds travel on the wind. Other fruits, such as coconuts and acorns, add weight so that the seeds will fall to the ground and roll away from the parent plant. Many plants have evolved to produce fruits that are tasty to birds and animals (and, often, to people as well). When creatures feast on these fruits, the seeds pass unharmed through their digestive systems. Later, the birds or animals discharge the seeds in their solid waste, perhaps far from the place where they ate the fruit.

In addition to reproducing sexually, many—but not all—plants can reproduce vegetatively. Some plants store food in underground organs called tubers, corms, or bulbs. New organs split off from these and then send out roots and shoots of their own, becoming independent new plants. Many plants also send out horizontal stems that put down new root systems. These are called runners when they are aboveground and rhizomes when they are belowground. If the connecting runner or rhizome is broken, each part of the plant continues to live independently. People use vegetative reproduction in a variety of ways. It is easier and faster to grow many garden plants, such as tulips and irises, from bulbs than from seeds. Cut branches or stems of many species of plants can also lend themselves to vegetative reproduction. If placed in water or a special type of soil called a growing medium, they form roots and eventually become complete plants. Gardeners and farmers use these techniques to duplicate plants that have desirable qualities.

GERMINATION AND GROWTH

Once a seed has landed in a favorable place, a new plant is ready to grow. The sprouting of a seed into a plant is called germination. It begins when conditions such as moisture level and temperature are just right for each species of plant. Water enters the seed, which swells. The seed coat splits, and

Germination occurs when a seed becomes a plant. Here an acorn, the seed of an oak tree, sends forth a hypocotyl, the downward-pointing root, and an epicotyl, the upward-pointing stem that is protected by two seed leaves.

the embryo begins to grow. One end of it, the hypocotyl, grows downward to become the beginning of the plant's root system. The other end, the epicotyl, grows upward. It is protected by either one or two small leaves, the cotyledons, that formed within the seed (monocots have one cotyledon; dicots have two). The cotyledons later unfold to reveal the tip of the plant's stem. As the stem continues to grow upward, the plant's first true leaves sprout from it.

An angiosperm's lifespan depends upon two factors: what kind of plant it is and its growing conditions. Each plant species has a typical lifespan that is determined by its genetic heritage. Many herbaceous plants are annuals (which live for one year or less) or biennials (which live for two years). Most annual or biennial plants reproduce only once. Other herbaceous plants have longer lifespans, as do nearly all trees. Plants that live for more than two years are called perennials. They typically produce seeds every year.

Even with the perfect amount of moisture, an ideal temperature, and rich soil, an annual plant will not live longer than a year. But poor conditions—such as a drought, a freeze, or an attack by disease or insect pests—can cut down any annual or perennial before its normal lifespan is complete. Dead plants remain part of the cycle of life, however. They provide food for hosts of small creatures such as insects, snails, and worms. Eventually they decompose, or break down into their basic elements, enriching the soil from which they sprang.

Gardeners often divide flowering plants into two categories based on their lifespans. Annuals, like the scarlet mallow (left) live for one year and usually reproduce once. Many annuals are prized as garden plants because of their colorful blooms. Perennials, such as the Central American *Anthurium trinerve* (above), live for more than two years. As trees, shrubs, or long-lasting plants, they form the structural backbones of many gardens.

The Madagascar periwinkle (*Caranthus roseus*, formerly called the rosy periwinkle or *Vinca rosea*) contains more than 70 chemicals called alkaloids that have medical uses. Two of them are effective in treating various kinds of cancer, including childhood leukemia and Hodgkin's lymphoma. Conservationists point to the benefits found in this single plant as an argument for protecting all species of angiosperms, many of which may hold undiscovered secrets.

The Role of Flowering Plants

Plants make animal life and human life possible. Without plants, we couldn't breathe or eat. From the uncountable numbers of microcopic plants that swirl in the ocean currents, to the tropical rain forests that are the home of the majority of the world's plant and animal species, to the fields upon fields of crops that feed the human population, plants are an essential part of earth's web of life. They are also the focus of much scientific activity—and, because most plants are flowering plants, the majority of plant research concerns angiosperms. Botanists and ecologists are scrambling to identify and study the vast number of species, while conservationists fight to protect flowering plants from threats such as habitat destruction, pollution, genetic damage, and extinction.

USES OF FLOWERING PLANTS

Many science-fiction writers have imagined how people could turn an alien planet into a suitable home for human beings. Some have used the word "terraforming" to describe the process of changing a planet's atmosphere, temperature, and other features to make it more like Terra, as Earth is sometimes called. Terraforming has already happened—right here on Terra. The habitable world we know was created in part by the activity of plants over millions of years. Their photosynthesis and respiration slowly but steadily changed the atmosphere, reducing carbon dioxide and increasing oxygen, producing the air we breathe today.

Plants also produce everything we eat. Grains, vegetables, and fruits come directly from plants. Meat and dairy products come from animals that eat plants. Some conservationists and activists working to combat hunger have called attention to the different demands that plant and meat foods make on the environment. They have compared the amounts of land and water needed to produce equal amounts of grain and beef, and they have also compared the effects of grain-farming and cattle-grazing on resources such as soil and streams. Researchers estimate that it costs anywhere from six to twenty times as much in resources to produce a pound of beef as it does to produce a pound of grain.

What would life be like without chocolate? Thanks to these cocoa beans, fruits of the cacao tree, we may never have to find out. Native to Central and South America, cacao trees are now grown in West Africa and elsewhere to feed the chocolate-hungry world.

In every part of the world, the basic or staple foods are the seeds of grain plants, chiefly wheat, rice, and corn. Tubers such as potatoes, yams, and cassava are also staples for millions of people. Other plant-based foods include vegetables, fruits, beans, nuts, oils (such as olive, vegetable, peanut, or sunflower oil), sugar, coffee, tea, chocolate, herbs (the leaves and stems of certain plants), and spices (made from seeds, flowers, fruits, and roots).

People have always used plants for much more than food. In many parts of the world people make houses, beds, clothing, and even boats from woven reeds and grasses. The ancient Eygptians wrote on papyrus, a paper-like material made from the pulp inside the stems of certain reeds; it is so durable that some fragments surviving today are three thousand years old. Much clothing is made from plant fibers, especially cotton and flax (linen is made from flax).

Papyrus reeds (left) grow in wet places, such as river deltas, in both northern and southern Africa. From papyrus the ancient Eygptians made a paper-like writing material. It was so durable that some pieces, such as this page from the Book of the Dead, found in the Valley of the Kings, have lasted for thousands of years.

After food, wood is the plant world's second most important contribution to human life and economy, although much of the timber that people harvest and use comes from conifers, not flowering trees. Buildings, boats, furniture, and countless smaller objects such as tool handles and toys are made of wood, as is paper. In many parts of the world, wood is the main fuel for cooking and heating. Another of the world's major fuels, coal, also comes from plants. It occurs where masses of plant material from ancient forests and swamps became buried in the earth. Over long periods of time, the weight of the land above pressed the plant matter into a burnable substance that resembles rock but is organic, not mineral. Because it consists of the remains of long-dead plants, coal is called a fossil fuel. Oil and natural gas, the other fossil fuels, are also created by pressure on the remains of ancient life forms, both plant and animal.

Many plants yield chemical substances that affect the human brain or body. Since ancient times people have used plants as medicines and intoxicants. For example, for hundreds of years people in many parts of the

Cimicifuga racemosa, or black cohosh, is one of many plants traditionally used in Native American medicines.

70

world have chewed willow bark to relieve pain. Today salicin, a chemical compound found in willow bark, is the basis of one of the most widely used drugs in the world: aspirin. Many other medicinal drugs are based on compounds from plants, often those used by traditional healers. Plants also produce alcohol, drugs such as marijuana, cocaine, and opium, and a wide variety of toxic compounds, or poisons.

Anyone who has ever taken care of a garden knows that unwanted plants can be most persistent. Infuriatingly, weeds may flourish even while expensive, well-tended plants wither and die. People tend to divide the plant world into useful or desirable species on one hand and weeds on the other. But as American writer Ralph Waldo Emerson pointed out, a weed is simply "a flower whose virtues have not yet been discovered." In the natural world there are no good plants and bad plants—there are simply different kinds of plants competing for survival.

THE CHALLENGE OF CONSERVATION

Botanists divide the world's plants into six general categories based on geography and climate, from holarctic in the far north to holantarctic in the far south. Within these broad categories, natural boundaries separate many different geographic regions, each with its own array of native plant species. The boundaries are not universal or clear-cut. Some plants found in the Saharo-Arabian region of North Africa, for example, are also found in the Mediterranean region. In general, though, the boundaries mark a shift from one flora, or assortment of life plant life, to another.

Although regional boundaries exist, plants have always crossed them, either naturally or by human design. In the modern world of global trade and travel, it is easier and more common than ever for seeds or other plant material to move from one part of the world to another. Sometimes people deliberately transport plants into new areas, often with unexpected results. The Asian vine called kudzu, for example, was introduced into the southern

PLANT COMMUNITIES OF THE WORLD

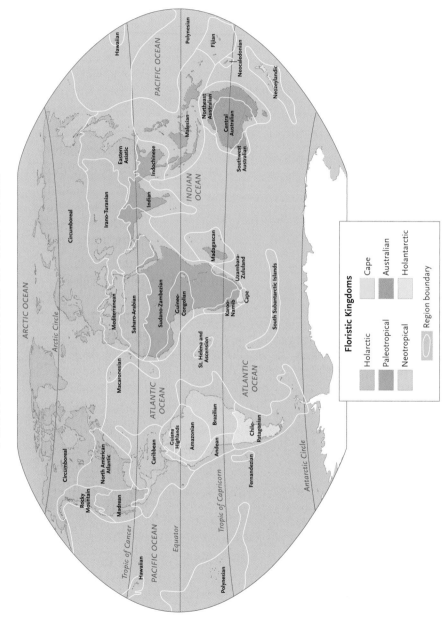

Floristic Kingdoms

- Holarctic
- Paleotropical
- Neotropical
- Cape
- Australian
- Holantarctic
- Region boundary

Botanists sometimes find it useful to look at plants in terms of their geographic distribution: how they are spread across the world. Scientists divide the world of angiosperms into six large realms called floristic (having to do with flowering) kingdoms. Certain kinds of plants are typical of each kingdom. Within the kingdoms are many smaller divisions called regions. Each region has characteristic groups of plant families. But the borders of plant geography are not hard and fast. Plants may become established in new regions after humans have transplanted them, for example, or climate change may shift the boundaries of floristic kingdoms and regions.

United States to control erosion and because people thought it might make a good cattle food. Kudzu never lived up to that promise, but it thrived and spread on American soil, becoming a tremendous nuisance because it does not die back every winter as in Japan. Other new plants have been introduced by accident, as when recreational boats carried the fast-growing aquatic plant called water hyacinth into lakes, rivers, and canals where it had not existed before. Newly introduced water hyacinth has clogged waterways, overwhelmed native plants, and harmed fish habitat in many places.

Plants that are not native to a region are called alien species. Some of them grow so well in their new territories that they eliminate native species—the newcomers are then called invasive species. Many environmental projects focus on removing invasive plants, but these intruders can be remarkably stubborn.

Water hyacinth, here growing in a stream in the Asian nation of Bangladesh, has become an invasive pest in the United States, where it is destroying native plant and animal life in some waterdays.

The Plant Pirates

For centuries travelers and explorers have brought new plants home from their journeys. Some of these botanical souvenirs have become prized garden plants, like the Himalayan rhododendrons that now bloom in gardens across North America and Great Britain every spring. Some plants reshaped eating habits or had other important economic effects. For example, people around the world now grow and eat American corn and tomatoes. In the mid-nineteenth century, two very valuable plants grew only in South America. One was the cinchona tree, whose bark yields quinine, a drug used to treat the widespread tropical disease malaria. The other was *Hevea brasiliensis*, a Brazilian tree whose sap, called latex, makes the best-quality rubber in the world. South American authorities were determined to prevent these profitable trees from being cultivated elsewhere. They were no match, however, for the resourceful plant collectors—or pirates, from the South American point of view—who smuggled cinchona and Brazilian rubber plants out of the continent.

In 1859 the British government hired Richard Spruce, an English botanist who had been collecting plants in South America for years, to obtain seeds and seedlings of the cinchona tree from the highlands of Ecuador. Spruce collected 100,000 seeds and hundreds of seedlings and carried them to the Pacific coast on a huge raft. Around the same time Clements Markham, a British traveler who later served as president of the Royal Geographical Society, gathered some cinchona seedlings in Peru. Both men managed to slip their booty past port authorities and ship it to India, where the British government established profitable cinchona plantations.

Latex sap drips from a tapped rubber tree trunk in the Asian nation of Malaysia. South America once controlled the rubber trade, until a British adventurer smuggled rubber tree seedlings out of Brazil for the British government.

A few years later the British government did the same thing for an even more valuable plant. Between 1850 and 1870 the price of Brazilian rubber had risen more than a hundredfold as industry found new uses for the versatile material. Tired of depending upon Brazil for latex, British officials turned to Henry Alexander Wickham, a traveler who had written a book about the Amazon rain forest. Through a combination of pluck and luck, Wickham managed to gather thousands of *H. brasiliensis* seeds, germinate them into seedlings, smuggle them down the Amazon River and past Brazilian officials, and keep them alive until they reached a botanical garden in London. From there the plants were sent to India. Before long, vast rubber plantations in Britain's Asian colonies ended Brazil's brief, glorious rubber boom.

Environmental threats to plants include acid rain, which occurs when harmful pollutants from automobile exhaust and industry contaminate the air and fall out of the atmosphere with rain.

Plant communities worldwide face threats other than invasive species. Climate change—the slight but definite warming of the world—is shrinking or enlarging the zones in which plants can grow. In North America and Eurasia, for example, some kinds of trees can grow farther north now than they could a century ago. At the same time, some small, hardy plants adapted to life in the cold northlands are retreating from the southern edges of their traditional zones. Some observers see these changes as the destructive results of human meddling with the global climate, while others view them as part of a natural cycle of changes in climate and vegetation.

Human activities do, however, have a powerful effect on plant life. Acid rain, which occurs when chemical pollution in the air falls to earth with rainwater, destroys chlorophyll, without which plants cannot manufacture food. Vegetation that has been heavily damaged by acid rain simply starves to death. Soil and water pollution by waste from mining, ranching, and industry can also harm plant life.

Modern, large-scale commercial agriculture has achieved remarkable successes in producing high crop yields. But those successes have come at a cost. To boost crop yields and protect crops from plant diseases and insect pests, many growers have relied more and more on chemical fertilizers and pesticides that contribute to soil and water pollution and, in some cases, can have harmful effects on the health of people who consume the crops. Another problem with large-scale commercial farming is that it encourages monoculture, which is the growing of a single crop and, often, a single variety of that crop. Some plant conservationists fear that the emphasis on a handful of commercially valuable crop varieties means that other varieties, scarcer and less widely used, may become extinct. The loss of these varieties could mean the loss of useful genetic qualities—features that could help a valuable species adapt to new conditions, such as new diseases. Around the world, botanical and agricultural research groups have founded gene banks to store seeds and conservation gardens to serve as homes for hundreds of fast-vanishing varieties of potatoes, tomatoes, corn, and other crops.

Modern large-scale farming has increased the food supply, but at a cost. By relying on chemical agents to fertilize soil and control pests, industrial farmers contribute to water and air pollution.

Dr. Dinie Espinal-Rueda of Honduras examines the stored tissue of an orchid. Espinal-Rueda, who started a program to save her nation's endangered national flower, is one of many scientists and activists worldwide who are working to preserve the genetic heritage of the plants that have shaped the world as we know it.

Gene banks, conservation gardens, and other protected places such as nature preserves and national parks may be some plants' best hopes for escaping extinction. As people clear land for building, farming, ranching, and logging, millions of acres each year lose their natural vegetation. Many species of plants have become extinct in modern times, and others are on the brink of disappearing, especially in the tropics. Some conservationists argue that we should protect and preserve as many plant species as possible because plants that are yet unknown may contain extremely useful substances, such as cures for deadly diseases. Yet practical concerns are not the only reasons for protecting the world's plant heritage. Plants, especially flowering plants, enrich the world with diversity, complexity, and sheer beauty, qualities worth preserving and passing on to future generations.

Visitors to a walkway through the canopy of the Monteverde Cloud Forest in Costa Rica get a bird's eye view of a high-altitude rain forest lush with hundreds of plant species. Some endangered plants, like some endangered animals, may be helped to survive by ecotourism, which allows visitors to marvel at the natural world's most diverse and precious angiosperm communities.

adapt—To change or develop in ways that aid survival in the environment.

algae—One-celled or multicelled plantlike organism generally found in water; usually classified in kingdom of protoctists, or protozoa.

anatomy—Internal structure.

ancestral—Having to do with lines of descent or earlier forms.

angiosperm—Flowering plant. The great majority of plants on earth, including grasses and most trees, are angiosperms.

annual—A plant that grows from seed, flowers, and dies within one year.

aquatic—Inhabiting fresh water.

conservation—Action or movement aimed at protecting and preserving wildlife or its habitat.

botany—Scientific study of plants.

evolution—Process by which new species, or types of plants and animals, emerge from old ones over time.

evolve—To change over time.

extinct—No longer existing; died out.

genetic—Having to do with genes, material made of DNA inside the cells of living organisms. Genes carry information about inherited characteristics from parents to offspring and determine the form of each organism.

germinate—To begin to grow.

herbaceous—Lacking woody or barklike tissue on stems and branches. Aboveground parts of herbaceous plants die during the winter.

marine—Inhabiting the ocean.

paleobotanist—A scientist who studies ancient or extinct plant life, usually through fossils.

perennial—A plant that lives for more than two years; usually flowers each year.

pesticide—A chemical that kills pests.

phloem—Specialized tissue that carries glucose made through photosynthesis from the plant's leaves to other parts of its structure.

photosynthesis—The process by which plants with specialized structures called chloroplasts in the cells of their leaves make food (in the form of the sugar glucose) from water, sunlight, and carbon dioxide.

plant—A multicelled organism made of complex cells (with a nucleus and other internal structures in each cell) that produces its own food through photosynthesis.

taxonomy—The scientific system for classifying living things, grouping them in categories according to similarities and differences, and naming them.

terrestrial—Inhabiting the land.

vascular—Having specialized tissues that allow water and nutrients to move through the plant's structure.

woody—Having woody or barklike tissue on stems and branches.

xylem—Specialized tissue that carries water upward from the plant's roots to its leaves.

DIVISION Magnoliophyta

CLASS Liliopsida (Monocots)

5 SUBCLASSES

Alismatids
4 Orders
Example: Arrowhead

Arecids
4 Orders
Examples: Palm, philodendron, duckweed

Commelinids
6 Orders
Examples: Rush, grass, cattail

Zingiberids
2 Orders
Example: Pineapple

Liliids
3 Orders
Examples: Lily, iris, orchid

FAMILY TREE

(all angiosperms)

CLASS Magnoliopsida (Dicots)

6 SUBCLASSES

Magnoliids
8 Orders
Examples: Magnolia, poppy

Hamamelid
11 Orders
Examples: Elm, oak, birch

Caryophyllids
3 Orders
Examples: Cactus, beet, buckwheat

Dilleniids
13 Orders
Examples: Willow, flytrap, cotton

Rosids
18 Orders
Examples: Mistletoe, maple, poison ivy

Asterids
11 Orders
Examples: Potato, mint, olive

F U R T H E R   R E A D I N G

Dowden, Anne. *From Flower to Fruit.* New York: Crowell, 1984.

—————. *The Clover and the Bee: A Book of Pollination.* New York: Crowell, 1990.

Forey, Pamela. *Wild Flowers of North America.* San Diego: Thunder Bay Press, 1994.

Ganeri, Anita. *What's Inside a Plant?* New York: Peter Bedrick Books, 1995.

Heller, Ruth. *The Reason for a Flower.* New York: Grosset & Dunlap, 1983.

Kite, Patricia. *Insect-Eating Plants.* Brookfield, CT: Millbrook Press, 1995.

Lauber, Patricia. *From Flower to Flower: Animals and Pollination.* New York: Crown, 1986.

Lerner, Carol. *Plant Families.* New York: Morrow Junior Books, 1989.

Leutscher, Alfred. *Flowering Plants.* New York: Franklin Watts, 1984.

Oppenheim, Joanne. *Floratorium.* New York: Bantam, 1994.

Platt, Richard. *Plants Bite Back!* New York: Dorling Kindersley, 1999.

The Visual Dictionary of Plants. New York: Dorling Kindersley, 1992.

Spiders and Flowers. Disney Educational Productions, 1996.

WEB SITES

waynesword.palomar.edu/trmar98/htm

Called Diversity of Flowering Plants, this site is part of a newletter of educational natural history trivia and has links to botany course notes that cover many topics of plant biology and ecology.

www.mobot.org

In addition to being a popular destination for visitors, the Missouri Botanical Garden is one of the world's leading centers of plant research, with an emphasis on tropical forests; its site has an educational section.

www.edenproject.com

In a huge crater in Cornwall, England, the Eden Project has created gardens of English, Mediterranean, South American, and tropical plants; the site offers a virtual tour and links to plant conservation information.

www.botany.com

Designed for gardeners and those seeking practical information about plants, this site, called Encyclopedia of Plants, features information about many species, listed under their scientific and common names.

The author found these books especially helpful when researching this volume.

Cronquist, Arthur. *An Integrated System of Classification of Flowering Plants.* New York: Columbia University Press, 1992.

Heywood, V.H. *Flowering Plants of the World.* New York: Oxford University Press, 1993.

Levetin, Estelle and Karen McMahon. *Plants and Society.* Dubuque, IA: Wm. C. Brown Publishers, 1996.

Meuse, Bastiaan and Sean Morris. *The Sex Life of Flowers.* New York: Facts On File, 1984.

Moore, David, editor. *Plant Life.* New York: Oxford University Press, 1991.

Musgrave, Toby, Chris Gardner, and Will Musgrave. *The Plant Hunters: Two Hundred Years of Adventure and Discovery Around the World.* London: Ward Lock, 1998.

Pearson, Lorentz C. *Diversity and Evolution of Plants.* Boca Raton, LA: CRC Press, 1995.

Willis, K.J. and J.C. McElwain. *The Evolution of Plants.* Oxford, England: Oxford University Press, 2002.

Zomlefer, Wendy B. *Guide to Families of Flowering Plants.* Raleigh-Durham: University of North Carolina Press, 1995.

I N D E X

Page numbers in **boldface** are illustrations and charts.

Rebecca Stefoff is the author of a number of books on scientific subjects for young readers. She has explored the world of animals in Marshall Cavendish's Living Things series and in the volumes *Horses, Bears, Dogs, Cats* and *Tigers* in the AnimalWays series, also published by Marshall Cavendish. She has also written about evolution in *Charles Darwin and the Evolution Revolution* (Oxford University Press, 1996), and she appeared in the *A&E Biography* segment on Charles Darwin and his work. Stefoff lives in Portland, Oregon. You can find out more about her and her books at www.rebeccastefoff.com